Shall I See You Again?

Shall I See You Again?

An Anthology of Love and the British

Edited by

Juliet Stevenson and Philip Franks

PAVILION

First published in Great Britain in 1993 by
Pavilion Books Limited
26 Upper Ground, London SE1 9PD

Selection copyright © 1993 by
Juliet Stevenson and Philip Franks

Designed by Atelier

A CIP catalogue record for this book is
available from the British Library

ISBN 1 85793 099 1

Printed and bound in Great Britain by Butler & Tanner Ltd.

2   4   6   8   10 9   7   5   3   1

This book may be ordered by post direct from
the publisher. Please contact the Marketing
Department. But try your bookshop first.

Contents

For
Michael Guy Stevens

Foreword

Juliet Stevenson

It is almost exactly a year since I sat with my father in his hospital room, talking of ways to raise money for the hospice where he worked as a volunteer. Two friends were with us, colleagues of my father's at St Wilfred's Hospice, and both great supporters, as he was, of their local theatre in Chichester. A happy idea was born – that I could perhaps cajole some actor friends into doing a one-off event at the theatre, which would involve the minimum of rehearsal and the maximum (hopefully) of bums on seats. My father had always hoped that I would do a season at Chichester Festival Theatre so that I could live at home for the summer and he could come to the show at least three times a week. In this I had so far let him down, so the idea seemed a good one on several counts: firstly, we could raise badly-needed funds for the hospice; secondly, he and my mother would at last get to see my friends and me traipsing the Chichester boards, albeit briefly; and thirdly, I privately hoped that this involvement in planning and organizing the event would offer him some diversion from the oppressive and consuming demands that his illness was making on his mind, body and spirit.

And so this anthology came into being, and on two of those three counts at least we were successful: both shows sold out, raising about £7,500 for the hospice; and Dad's contribution to, and excitement about, the impending event served, in some measure, to alleviate his preoccupation with what lay in store for him. Sadly, on one count things did not work out as we had hoped: his desire to see us all perform at his much-loved local theatre was not fulfilled, as he did not live to see the show. His illness escalated rapidly in the interim, the cancer charting its unpredictable and uncontainable course, and he died on 21 June.

The show was performed on 2 August 1992. It was dedicated to him and to his work for the hospice, and was attended by many of his friends and colleagues. The anthology contained many of his favourites: extracts from plays he had most loved seeing; poems he had known off by heart since childhood; sketch material he had not known but which would have made him roar with laughter – and somehow the spirit of the event became infused with his own. He was, in that sense, present.

The publication of the anthology now extends the offering to him, and in addition will hopefully raise money for research into the disease which took him away, as it does so many. It remains only for me to thank several people for their help along the way: Patrick Garland for enabling and directing us; Gillian Plowman and Maddy Boyce at St Wilfred's Hospice for their support and contributions; Liora Lazarus for her patience and her powers at the word-processor; my friends Philip Franks, Alan Rickman and Paola Dionisotti for a weekend of sweat, insomnia, spirit and skill; my mother, Virginia, for housing us, feeding us, last-minute ironing and continual encouragement; and thanks, above all, to my father, for everything I owe him.

Juliet Stevenson,
London 1993

Foreword

Philip Franks

The anthology you are about to read is based on two performances given in August 1992 at the Minerva Studio, Chichester. These performances were planned well in advance and the scripts were written, typed out and rehearsed in a blind panic at the last minute. Juliet and I had exchanged many inconclusive phone calls, the gist of each being 'we really must get down to doing the anthology'. Somehow that seemed to be enough, and neither of us really did anything about it beyond securing the services of Alan Rickman and Paola Dionisotti and fobbing off the Chichester Festival Theatre with bland reassurances. We panicked briefly when we heard that both scheduled performances were sold out, but the real work was done over three long days leading up to the Sunday of the show.

The first day was spent in my flat with Juliet and Paola, assembling the show, deciding on the format, content and nature of the piece. This involved much diplomacy, some confusion ('why on earth has he chosen *that*?') and a certain amount of hilarity and stress. The second – an unhelpfully hot day – involved Juliet and myself sweating over an illegally 'borrowed' photocopier in a tiny office in Bloomsbury with a patient friend hammering away at a word processor in the corner. The third was an all-nighter in the conservatory at Juliet's mother's house near Chichester. At some point during those three days we must have managed about five hours' sleep but I don't remember them too clearly.

We performed the anthology under the title *The British in Love*. This needs some explanation. Patrick Garland, Chichester's Artistic Director, as well as generously donating the theatre, had suggested we perform an evening based on Jilly Cooper's well-known anthology, which he and others had already presented in various forms over the last few years with great success. When we read this script, however, we decided that, although charming and witty, it did not quite fit the personalities involved. What started as an attempt to slide in the odd new or favourite extract led to an unpicking of the whole programme.

There are of course some pieces from the original anthology that were too good to waste and we include them here, with thanks to Jilly Cooper and Patrick Garland for introducing us to them. The desire to have a close look at how the British as a race (if they are one, and not a random collection of contradictions) deal with love, finding it, keeping it, abusing it and losing it, is a desire which our anthology shares with the previous one. In the main, however, this is a reconstruction job, and it is greatly to Patrick's credit that he didn't turn a hair when a show twice as long as, and totally different from, the one he was expecting turned up in his theatre on the Sunday morning.

The Minerva Studio is an intimate three-sided auditorium with great possibilities for audience contact. We decided to abandon the traditional staging of such pieces – four chairs in a row and a lectern, with the readers in formal dress – in favour of flinging ourselves around a bit. Pieces were done on foot, running around, on the floor or even lying flat. The show could be done in a more static way but I would encourage anyone performing it to be as irreverent as possible. It worked very well with the enthusiastic audiences, and to me at least seemed an appropriate tribute to Mike Stevens, a man of great enthusiasm, openness, good humour and courage.

Philip Franks,
London 1993

Royalties from the sale of this edition will be donated to the Imperial Cancer Research Fund.

 **Imperial Cancer**
Research Fund
Registered Charity Number 209631

Prologue

from Brief Encounter
Noël Coward (1899–1972)

> (*Laura and Alec are having tea in the waiting-room of a suburban railway station.*)

LAURA   Is tea bad for one? Worse than coffee, I mean?

ALEC   If this is a professional interview, my fee is a guinea.

LAURA   Why did you become a doctor?

ALEC   That's a long story. Perhaps because I'm a bit of an idealist.

LAURA   I suppose all doctors ought to have ideals, really – otherwise I should think their work would be unbearable.

ALEC   Surely you're not encouraging me to talk shop?

LAURA   Why shouldn't you talk shop? It's what interests you most, isn't it?

ALEC   Yes, it is. I'm terribly ambitious really, not ambitious for myself so much as for my special pigeon.

LAURA   What is your special pigeon?

ALEC   Preventative medicine.

LAURA   Oh, I see.

ALEC   (*laughing*) I'm afraid you don't.

LAURA   I was trying to be intelligent.

ALEC   Most good doctors, especially when they're young, have private dreams – that's the best part of them; sometimes, though, those get overprofessionalised and strangulated and – am I boring you?

LAURA   No – I don't quite understand – but you're not boring me.

ALEC   What I mean is this – all good doctors must be primarily enthusiastic. They must have, like writers and painters and priests, a sense of vocation – a deep-rooted, unsentimental desire to do good.

LAURA   Yes – I see that.

ALEC   Well, obviously one way of preventing disease is worth fifty ways of curing it – that's where my ideal comes in – preventative medicine isn't anything to do with medicine at all, really – it's concerned with conditions, living conditions and common sense and hygiene. For instance, my speciality is pneumoconiosis.

LAURA   Oh dear!

ALEC   Don't be alarmed, it's simpler than it sounds – it's nothing but a slow process of fibrosis of the lung due to the inhalation of particles of dust. In the hospital here there are splendid opportunities for observing cures and making notes, because of the coal-mines.

LAURA   You suddenly look much younger.

ALEC   *(brought up short)* Do I?

LAURA   Almost like a little boy.

ALEC   What made you say that?

LAURA   *(staring at him)* I don't know – yes, I do.

ALEC   *(gently)* Tell me.

LAURA   *(with panic in her voice)* Oh no – I couldn't really. You were saying about the coal-mines.

ALEC   *(looking into her eyes)* Yes – the inhalation of coaldust – that's one specific form of the disease – it's called anthracosis.

LAURA   *(hypnotised)* What are the others?

ALEC   Chalicosis – that comes from metal-dust – steelworks, you know. . .

LAURA   Yes, of course. Steel-works.

ALEC   And silicosis – stone-dust – that's gold-mines.

LAURA   *(almost in a whisper)* I see.
         (There is the sound of a bell.)

LAURA   That's your train.

ALEC   *(looking down)* Yes.

LAURA   You mustn't miss it.

ALEC   No.

LAURA   *(again with panic in her voice)* What's the matter?

ALEC   *(with an effort)* Nothing – nothing at all.

LAURA   *(socially)* It's been so very nice – I've enjoyed my afternoon enormously.

ALEC   I'm so glad – so have I. I apologise for boring you with those long medical words.

LAURA   I feel dull and stupid, not to be able to understand more.

ALEC   Shall I see you again?

(There is the sound of a train approaching.)

LAURA   It's the other platform, isn't it? You'll have to run.
         Don't worry about me – mine's due in a few minutes.

ALEC   Shall I see you again?

LAURA   Of course – perhaps you could come over to
         Ketchworth one Sunday. It's rather far, I know, but we
         should be delighted to see you.

ALEC   *(intensely)* Please – please. . .

         (The train is heard drawing to a standstill. . .)

LAURA   What is it?

ALEC   Next Thursday – the same time.

LAURA   No – I can't possibly – I. . .

ALEC ·   Please – I ask you most humbly. . .

LAURA   You'll miss your train!

ALEC   All right. *(He gets up)*

LAURA   Run. . .

ALEC   *(taking her hand)* Good-bye.

LAURA   *(breathlessly)* I'll be there.

ALEC   Thank you, my dear.

from Young Love: One
Victoria Wood

         *(Carl and Gail are a slow-witted Northern pair, sitting on a wall
         because they can't think of anywhere to go.)*

GAIL   Do you love me, Carl?

CARL   Yeah, you're all right.

GAIL   Do you think about me when you're cleaning windows?

CARL   Yeah, some of the time.

GAIL   Do you think about me when you're having your dinner?

CARL   Depends what it is.

GAIL   What do you mean, Carl?

CARL   I might if I'm having a Scotch egg, but if I'm having
         crisps, I'm concentrating on opening t'bag, aren't I?

GAIL   What about at night?

CARL   What about at night?

GAIL   Do you think about me then?

CARL In bed?

GAIL Yeah, or under it.

CARL When I'm in bed, Gail, I'm reading *The Puzzler*, aren't I?

GAIL Yeah, but, when your mam's put light out, and you've just closed your eyes, what do you think about then, Carl?

CARL My shammy leather.

(Pause.)

GAIL When we get married, Carl, where will we live?

CARL Well, we're living in my mam's sideboard, aren't we?

GAIL Yeah, but after that. Shall we have an 'ouse?

CARL Nah. Penthouse flat.

GAIL What's that, Carl?

CARL It's got fur rugs, hasn't it?

GAIL What colour?

CARL Well, it depends, dunnit? If it's off an animal, it'll be animal-coloured, won't it? Or there's orange.

GAIL Where is it?

CARL What?

GAIL This flat.

CARL Well, they're all in London, aren't they? And there's two in the Isle of Man.

GAIL Is that the same as France?

CARL France is abroad isn't it? They have different bread and allsorts.

GAIL Different allsorts? You mean not liquorice?

CARL Eh? Anyway, they're on t'roof.

GAIL What?

CARL Penthouse flats.

GAIL I'm not living on a roof. My knitting'll roll into t'guttering.

CARL Who's been telling you about guttering?

GAIL You did. When we were kissing goodnight last night, and we snuggled up, and you said you had something to tell me, and you told me about guttering.

CARL Yeah, well, I won't always be that romantic.

GAIL OK Carl.

Those two pieces conform to our most clichéd preconceptions of how the British behave when they are in love, from stiff upper lips, moist eyes and hearts breaking silently over teacups, to damp anoraks and a shared bag of humbugs at the bus stop. But of course, like all preconceptions, this reflects only a fraction of the truth. Listen to Emily Brontë and John Keats.

from Wuthering Heights
Emily Brontë (1818–1848)

Nelly, if I were in heaven I should be extremely miserable. I dreamed once that I was there and it did not seem to be my home; and I broke my heart with weeping to come back to earth: and the angels were so angry that they flung me out into the middle of the heath on the top of Wuthering Heights; where I woke sobbing for joy. That will do to explain my secret, as well as the other. I've no more business to marry Edgar Linton than I have to be in heaven: and if the wicked man in there hadn't brought Heathcliff so low, I shouldn't have thought of it. It would degrade me to marry Heathcliff now: so he shall never know how I love him: and that, not because he's handsome Nelly but because he's more myself than I am. Whatever our souls are made of his and mine are the same, and Linton's is as different as a moonbeam from lightning or frost from fire.

My great miseries in this world have been Heathcliff's miseries, and I watched and felt each from the beginning: my great thought in living is himself. If all else perished and *he* remained, *I* should still continue to be; if all else remained and he were annihilated, the universe would turn to a mighty stranger: I should not seem a part of it. My love for Linton is like the foliage in the woods: time will change it, I'm well aware, as winter changes the trees. My love for Heathcliff resembles the eternal rocks beneath: a source of little visible delight but necessary. Nelly I *am* Heathcliff! He's always, always in my mind: not as a pleasure, any more than I am always a pleasure to myself, but as my own being. So don't talk of our separating again – it is impracticable.

Letter to Fanny Brawne

John Keats (1795–1821)

I see life in nothing but the certainty of your love – convince me
of it my sweetheart. If I am not somehow convinced I shall die of
agony. If we love we must not live as other men and women do. I
cannot brook the wolfsbane of fashion and foppery and tattle.
You must be mine to die upon the rack if I want you. No – my
sweet Fanny – I am wrong. I do not want you to be unhappy –
and yet I do, I must while there is so sweet a Beauty – my
loveliest, my darling! Goodbye! I kiss you – O, the torments!

J. K.

*So, if the British in love can be as irrepressibly passionate as they are
passionately repressed, there's no easy pigeon-holing. The journey of our
anthology is now going loosely to follow a journey through life, from
childhood and first love, through to the grave and beyond, hopefully
exploring chaos, contrasts and contradictions along the way. We start
with two poems. The second – a great favourite of the man to whom this
book is dedicated – is by Charles Stuart Calverley, the unjustly neglected
nineteenth-century classicist; the first, is by Katherine Mansfield.*

Part One

Childhood, Adolescence and First Love

There was a Child Once
Katherine Mansfield (1888–1923)

There was a child once
He came to play in my garden;
He was quite pale and silent.
Only when he smiled I knew everything about him,
I knew what he had in his pockets,
And I knew the feel of his hands in my hands
And the most intimate tones of his voice.
I led him down each secret path,
Showing him the hiding place of all my treasures.
I let him play with them every one,
I put my singing thoughts in a little silver cage
And gave them to him to keep. . .
It was very dark in the garden
But never dark enough for us. On tiptoe we walked among the
    deepest shades;
We bathed in the shadow pools beneath the trees,
Pretending we were under the sea.
Once – near the boundary of the garden –
We heard steps passing along the World-road;
Oh how frightened we were!

WISHING YOU A HAPPY CHRISTMAS

I whispered: have you ever walked along that road?
He nodded, and we shook the tears from our eyes. . .
There was a child once
He came – quite alone – to play in my garden
He was pale and silent
When we met we kissed each other,
But when he went away, we did not even wave.

Gemini and Virgo

Charles Stuart Calverley (1831–1884)

Some vast amounts of years ago,
    Ere all my youth had vanish'd from me
A boy it was my lot to know,
    Whom his familiar friends called Tommy.

I love to gaze upon a child;
    A young bud bursting into blossom;
Artless, as Eve yet unbeguiled,
    And agile as a young opossum;

And such was he. A calm-brow'd lad,
    Yet mad, at moments, as a hatter:
Why hatters as a race are mad
    I never knew, nor does it matter.

He was what nurses call a 'limb';
    One of those small misguided creatures,
Who, tho' their intellects are dim,
    Are one too many for their teachers:

And, if you asked of him to say
    What twice 10 was, or 3 times 7,
He'd glance (in quite a placid way)
    From heaven to earth, from earth to heaven;

And smile, and look politely round,
    To catch a casual suggestion;
But make no effort to propound
    Any solution of the question.

And so not much esteemed was he
    Of the authorities: and therefore
He fraternized by chance with me,
    Needing a somebody to care for:

And three fair summers did we twain
      Live (as they say) and love together;
And bore by turns the wholesome cane
      Till our young skins became as leather:

And carved our names on every desk,
      And tore our clothes, and inked our collars;
And looked unique and picturesque,
But not, it may be, model scholars.

We did much as we chose to do;
      We'd never heard of Mrs Grundy;
All the theology we knew
      Was that we mightn't play on Sunday;

And all the general truths, that cakes
      Were to be bought at four a penny,
And that excruciating aches
      Resulted if we ate too many.

And seeing ignorance is bliss,
      And wisdom consequently folly,
The obvious result is this –
      That our two lives were very jolly.

At last the separation came.
      Real love, at that time, was the fashion;
And by a horrid chance, the same
      Young thing was, to us both, a passion.

Old POSER snorted like a horse:
      His feet were large, his hands were pimply,
His manner, when excited, coarse:
      But Miss P. was an angel simply.

She was a blushing, gushing thing;
        All – more than all – my fancy painted;
Once – when she helped me to a wing
        Of goose – I thought I should have fainted.

The people said that she was blue:
        But I was green, and loved her dearly.
She was approaching thirty-two;
        And I was then eleven, nearly.

I did not love as others do;
        (None ever did that I've heard tell of;)
My passion was a byword through
        The town she was, of course, the belle of.

Oh sweet – as to the toilworn man
        The far-off sound of rippling river;
As to cadets in Hindostan
        The fleeting remnant of their liver-

To me was ANNA; dear as gold
        That fills the miser's sunless coffers;
As to the spinster, growing old,
        The thought – the dream – that she had offers.

I'd sent her little gifts of fruit;
        I'd written lines to her as Venus;
I'd sworn unflinchingly to shoot
        The man who dared to come between us:

And it was you, my Thomas, you,
        The friend in whom my soul confided,
Who dared to gaze on her – to do,
        I may say, much the same as I did.

One night, I *saw* him squeeze her hand;
    There was no doubt about the matter;
I said he must resign, or stand
    My vengeance – and he chose the latter.

We met, we 'planted' blows on blows:
    We fought as long as we were able:
My rival had a bottle-nose,
    And both my speaking eyes were sable,

When the school-bell cut short our strife,
    Miss P. gave both of us a plaister;
And in a week became the wife
    Of Horace Nibbs, the writing-master.

I loved her then – I'd love her still,
    Only one must not love Another's:
But thou and I, my Tommy, will,
    When we again meet, meet as brothers.

It may be that in age one seeks
        Peace only: that the blood is brisker
In boys' veins, than in theirs whose cheeks
        Are partially obscured by whisker;

Or that the growing ages steal
        The memories of past wrongs from us.
But this is certain – that I feel
        Most friendly unto thee, oh Thomas!

And whereso'er we meet again,
        On this or that side the equator,
If I've not turned teetotaller then,
        And have wherewith to pay the waiter,

To thee I'll drain the modest cup,
        Ignite with thee the mild Havannah;
And we will waft, while liquoring up,
        Forgiveness to the heartless ANNA.

From childhood to adolescence; young people
'standing tiptoe on the edge of life'. In a moment,
Stella Gibbons' heroine, Flora, casting a cold eye
at what's on offer. First, Shakespeare's Juliet in
altogether more receptive mode.

from Romeo and Juliet

William Shakespeare (1564–1616)

Act III scene ii

> *(A room in Capulet's house.)*
> *(Enter Juliet.)*

JULIET   Gallop apace, you fiery-footed steeds,
Towards Phoebus' lodging: such a waggoner
As Phaeton would whip you to the west,
And bring in cloudy night immediately.
Spread thy close curtain, love-performing night,
That runaways' eyes may wink, and Romeo
Leap to these arms, untalk'd of and unseen.
Lovers can see to do their amorous rites
By their own beauties; or, if love be blind,
It best agrees with night. – Come, evil night,
Thou sober-suited matron, all in black,
And learn me how to lose a winning match,
Play'd for a pair of stainless maidenhoods:
Hood my unmann'd blood, bating in my cheeks,
With thy black mantle; till strange love grown bold,
Think true love acted simple modesty.
Come, night; come, Romeo, – come, thou day in night;
For thou wilt lie upon the wings of night
Whiter than snow upon a raven's back.–
Come, gentle night; come, loving, black-brow'd night,
Give me my Romeo; and, when he shall die,
Take him and cut him out in little stars,
And he will make the face of heaven so fine,
That all the world will be in love with night,
And pay no worship to the garish sun.
O, I have bought the mansion of a love,
But not possess'd it; and, though I am sold,
Not yet enjoy'd: so tedious is this day,
As is the night before some festival
To an impatient child, that hath new robes,
And may not wear them. O, here comes my nurse,
And she brings news; and every tongue, that speaks
But Romeo's name, speaks heavenly eloquence.

But, of course, first encounters are not always so rapturous, nor so mutual. Flora's experience in Cold Comfort Farm *is altogether different.*

from Cold Comfort Farm
Stella Gibbons (1902–1989)

It cannot be said that Flora really enjoyed taking walks with Mr Mybug. To begin with, he was not really interested in anything but sex. This was understandable, if deplorable. After all, many of our best minds have had the same weakness. The trouble about Mr Mybug was that ordinary objects, which are not usually associated with sex even by our best minds, did suggest sex to Mr Mybug, and he pointed them out and made comparisons and asked Flora what she thought about it all. Flora found it difficult to reply because she was not interested. She was therefore obliged merely to be polite, and Mr Mybug mistook her lack of enthusiasm and thought it was due to inhibitions. He remarked how curious it was that most Englishwomen (most young Englishwomen, that was, Englishwomen of about nineteen to twenty-four) were inhibited. Cold, that was what young Englishwomen from nineteen to twenty-four were.

They used sometimes to walk through a pleasant wood of young birch trees which were just beginning to come into bud. The stems reminded Mr Mybug of phallic symbols and the buds made Mr Mybug think of nipples and virgins. Mr Mybug pointed out to Flora that he and she were walking on seeds which were germinating in the womb of the earth. He said it made him feel as if he were trampling on the body of a great brown woman. He felt as if he were a partner in some mighty rite of gestation.

Flora used sometimes to ask him the name of a tree, but he never knew.

Yet there were occasions when he was not reminded of a pair of large breasts by the distant hills. Then, he would stand looking at the woods upon the horizon. He would wrinkle up his eyes and breathe deeply through his nostrils and say that the view

reminded him of one of Poussin's lovely things. Or he would pause and peer in a pool and say it was like a painting by Manet.

And, to be fair to Mr Mybug, it must be admitted he was sometimes interested by the social problems of the day. Only yesterday, while he and Flora were walking through an alley of rhododendrons on an estate which was open to the public, hehad discussed a case of arrest in Hyde Park. The rhododendrons made him think of Hyde Park. He said it was impossible to sit down for five minutes in Hyde Park after seven o'clock in the evening without being either accosted or arrested.

There were many homosexuals to be seen in Hyde Park. Prostitutes, too. God! those rhododendron buds had a phallic, urgent look!

Sooner or later we should have to tackle the problem of homosexuality. We should have to tackle the problem of lesbians and old maids.

God! that little pool down there in the hollow was shaped just like somebody's navel! He would like to drag off his clothes and leap into it. There was another problem. . . We should have to tackle that, too. In no other country but England was there so much pruriency about nakedness. If we all went about naked, sexual desire would automatically disappear. Had Flora ever been to a party where everybody took off all their clothes? Mr Mybug had. Once a whole lot of us bathed in the river with nothing on and afterwards little Harriet Belmont sat naked in the grass and played to us on her flute. It was delicious; so gay and simple and natural. And Billie Polswett danced a Hawaiian love-dance, making all the gestures that are usually omitted in the stage version. Her husband had danced too. It had been lovely; so warm and natural and *real*, somehow.

So, taking it all round, Flora was pleased to have her walk in solitude.

Flora wisely opts for caution in dealing with the priapic Mr Mybug. But caution can be an enemy as well as a friend – two of Shakespeare's most famous lovers are nearly undone by it at the outset. In a neat subversion of conventional roles, it is Orlando who is blushing and tongue-tied in the company of the more forward Rosalind . . .

from As You Like It

William Shakespeare (1564–1616)
Act I scene ii

ROSALIND (*taking a chain from her neck*) Gentleman,
            Wear this for me; one out of suits with fortune
            That could give more but that her hand lacks means.
            Shall we go, coz?

CELIA   Ay. Fare you well, fair gentleman.

ORLANDO   Can I not say, 'I thank you'? My better parts
            Are all thrown down, and that which here stands up
            Is but a quintain, a mere lifeless block.

ROSALIND He calls us back. My pride fell with my fortunes;
            I'll ask him what he would. Did you call, sir?
            Sir, you have wrestled well, and overthrown
            More than your enemies.

CELIA   Will you go, coz?

ROSALIND Have with you. Fare you well.
                            (*Exeunt Rosalind and Celia*)

ORLANDO   What passion hangs these weights upon my tongue?
            I cannot speak to her, yet she urged conference.
            O poor Orlando, thou art overthrown!
            Or Charles, or something weaker masters thee.

> *But Rosalind and Orlando have a whole play
> ahead of them to sort things out. Missed
> opportunities have a darker consequence in the
> next poem. 'The Cap and Bells' perhaps had a
> particular resonance for its author W. B. Yeats,
> who spent much of his adult life carrying a torch
> for the unyielding Maud Gonne. Yeats was not
> British, but we wanted to include him.*

'The Cap and Bells'

W. B. Yeats (1865–1939)

The jester walked in the garden:
The garden had fallen still;
He bade his soul rise upward
and stand on her window-sill.

It rose in a straight blue garment,
When owls began to call:
It had grown wise-tongued by thinking
Of a quiet and light footfall;

But the young queen would not listen;
She rose in her pale nightgown;
She drew in the heavy casement
And pushed the latches down.

He bade his heart go to her,
When the owls called out no more;
In a red and quivering garment
It sang to her through the door.

It had grown sweet-tongued by dreaming
Of a flutter of flower-like hair;
But she took up her fan from the table
And waved it off on the air.

'I have cap and bells', he pondered,
'I will send them to her and die';
And when the morning whitened
He left them where she went by.

She laid them upon her bosom,
Under a cloud of her hair,
And her red lips sang them a love-song
Till stars grew out of the air.

She opened her door and her window,
And the heart and the soul came through
To her right hand came the red one,
To her left hand came the blue.

And they set up a noise like crickets,
A chattering wise and sweet,
And her hair was a folded flower
And the quiet of love in her feet.

Even if opportunities are not missed, first encounters between prospective lovers are not necessarily harmonious . . .

from The Taming of the Shrew

William Shakespeare (1564–1616)

Act II scene i

PETRUCHIO   Good morrow, Kate – for that's your name, I hear.

KATHERINA   Well have you heard, but something hard of
        hearing:
    They call me Katherine that do talk of me.

PETRUCHIO   You lie, in faith, for you are called plain Kate,
    And bonny Kate, and sometimes Kate the curst.
    But Kate, the prettiest Kate in Christendom,
    Kate of Kate Hall, my super-dainty Kate,
    For dainties are all Kates, and therefore, Kate,
    Take this of me, Kate of my consolation –
    Hearing thy mildness praised in every town,
    Thy virtues spoke of, and thy beauty sounded,
    Yet not so deeply as to thee belongs,
    Myself am moved to woo thee for my wife.

KATHERINA   Moved, in good time! Let him that moved you
        hither
    Remove you hence. I knew you at the first
    You were a movable.

PETRUCHIO   Why, what's a movable?

KATHERINA   A joint-stool.

PETRUCHIO   Thou hast hit it. Come, sit on me.

KATHERINA   Asses are made to bear, and so are you.

PETRUCHIO   Women are made to bear, and so are you.

KATHERINA   No such jade as you, if me you mean.

PETRUCHIO   Alas, good Kate, I will not burden thee!
    For knowing thee to be but young and light –

KATHERINA   Too light for such a swain as you to catch,
    And yet as heavy as my weight should be.

PETRUCHIO   Should be? Should – buzz!

KATHERINA   Well ta'en, and like a
        buzzard.

PETRUCHIO   O slow-winged turtle, shall a buzzard take thee?

KATHERINA   Ay, for a turtle, as he takes a buzzard.

PETRUCHIO   Come, come, you wasp, i'faith, you are too angry.

KATHERINA   If I be waspish, best beware my sting.

PETRUCHIO   My remedy is then to pluck it out.

KATHERINA   Ay, if the fool could find it where it lies.

PETRUCHIO   Who knows not where a wasp does wear his sting?

KATHERINA   In his tongue.

PETRUCHIO   Whose tongue?

KATHERINA   Yours, if you talk of tales, and so farewell.

(She turns to go.)

PETRUCHIO   What, with my tongue in your tail? Nay come
            again.

(He takes her in his arms.)

            Good Kate, I am a gentleman –

KATHERINA   That I'll try.

(She strikes him.)

PETRUCHIO   I swear I'll cuff you, if you strike again.

KATHERINA   So may you loose your arms.
            If you strike me, you are no gentleman,
            And if no gentleman, why then no arms

PETRUCHIO   A herald, Kate? O, put me in thy books

KATHERINA   What is your crest – a coxcomb?

PETRUCHIO   A combless cock, so Kate will be my hen.

KATHERINA   No cock of mine, you crow too like a craven.

PETRUCHIO   Nay, come, Kate, come, you must not look so sour.

KATHERINA   It is my fashion when I see a crab.

PETRUCHIO   Why, here's no crab, and therefore look not sour.

KATHERINA   There is, there is.

PETRUCHIO   Then show it me.

KATHERINA   Had I a glass, I would.

PETRUCHIO   What, you mean my face?

KATHERINA   Well aim'd of such a
            young one.

PETRUCHIO   Now, by Saint George, I am too young for you.

KATHERINA   Yet you are withered.

PETRUCHIO   'Tis with cares.

KATHERINA   I care not.

PETRUCHIO   Nay, hear you, Kate –

(She struggles.)

                              In sooth, you scape not so.

KATHERINA   I chafe you, if I tarry. Let me go.

Vows

The first hurdles surmounted, love is in the air. And once you have been bitten by the bug of romantic love, it is almost impossible to keep your feelings in check. But what do we mean *by the vows that we swear to each other so ardently? As W. H. Auden said:*

"'I will love you for ever"' swears the poet. I find this easy to swear too. "I will love you at 4.15 p.m. next Tuesday": is that still as easy?

"'I will love you whatever happens, even though you put on 20 pounds, or become afflicted with a moustache" – dare I promise that?'

from Troilus and Cressida

William Shakespeare (1564–1616)

Act III scene ii

TROILUS   O that I thought it could be in a woman –
As, if it can, I will presume in you –
To feed for aye her lamp and flames of love;
To keep her constancy in plight and youth,
Outliving beauty's outward, with a mind
That doth renew swifter than blood decays;
That my integrity and truth to you
Might be affronted with the match and weight
Of such a winnowed purity in love:
How were I then uplifted! But, alas,
I am as true as truth's simplicity,
And simpler than the infancy of truth.

CRESSIDA   In that I'll war with you.

TROILUS   O virtuous fight,
                When right with right wars who shall be most right!
                True swains in love shall in the world to come
                Approve their truth by Troilus. When their rhymes,
                Full of protest, of oath and big compare,
                Wants similes, truth tired with iteration,
                "As true as steel, as plantage to the moon,
                As sun to day, as turtle to her mate,
                As iron to adamant, as earth to the center,"
                Yet, after all comparisons of truth,
                As truth's authentic author to be cited,
                "As true as Troilus" shall crown up the verse
                And sanctify the numbers.

CRESSIDA   Prophet may you be!
                If I be false or swerve a hair from truth,
                When time is old and hath forgot itself,
                When waterdrops have worn the stones of Troy,
                And blind oblivion swallowed cities up,
                And mighty states characterless are grated
                To dusty nothing, yet let memory,
                From false to false among false maids in love,
                Upbraid my falsehood! When they've said, "As false
                As air, as water, wind or sandy earth,
                As fox to lamb, as wolf to heifer's calf,
                Pard to the hind, or stepdame to her son,"
                Yea, let them say, to stick the heart of falsehood,
                "As false as Cressid."

He wishes for the Cloths of Heaven
W. B. Yeats (1865–1939)

Had I the heavens' embroidered cloths,
Enwrought with golden and silver light,
The blue and the dim and the dark cloths
Of night and light and the half-light,
I would spread the cloths under your feet:
But I, being poor, have only my dreams;
I have spread my dreams under your feet;
Tread softly because you tread on my dreams.

from As You Like It

William Shakespeare (1564–1616)

Act IV scene i

ROSALIND   Am not I your Rosalind?

ORLANDO   I take some joy to say you are, because I would be talking of her.

ROSALIND   Well, in her person, I say I will not have you.

ORLANDO   Then in mine own person I die.

ROSALIND   No, faith, die by attorney. The poor world is almost six thousand years old, and in all this time there was not any man died in his own person, videlicet, in a love-cause. Troilus had his brains dashed out with a Grecian club, yet he did what he could to die before, and he is one of the patterns of love. Leander, he would have lived many a fair year though Hero had turned nun, if it had not been for a hot midsummer night; for, good youth, he went but forth to wash him in the Hellespont, and being taken with the cramp, was drowned, and the foolish chroniclers of that age found it was Hero of Sestos. But these are all lies: men have died from time to time and worms have eaten them, but not for love.

ORLANDO   I would not have my right Rosalind of this mind, for I protest her frown might kill me.

ROSALIND   By this hand, it will not kill a fly. But come, now I will be your Rosalind in a more coming-on disposition; and ask me what you will, I will grant it.

ORLANDO   Then love me Rosalind.

ROSALIND   Yes faith will I, Fridays and Saturdays and all.

Going Right

*Although Rosalind has poured refreshing cold
water on romantic clichés, when she enters her
'coming-on disposition' the sun comes out and,
as e. e. cummings says, 'flowers pick themselves'.
We are entering the sunny world of
unadulterated joy, at least for a while. Like any
new world, it must be thoroughly explored.*

Silent Noon

(Sonnet XIX)
Dante Gabriel Rossetti (1828–1882)

Your hands lie open in the long fresh grass, –
The finger-prints look through like rosy blooms:
Your eyes smile peace. The pasture gleams and glooms
'Neath billowing skies that scatter and amass.
All round our nest, far as the eye can pass,
Are golden kingcup-fields with silver edge
Where the cow-parsley skirts the hawthorn-hedge.
'Tis visible silence, still as the hour-glass.

Deep in the sun-searched growths the dragon-fly
Hangs like a blue thread loosened from the sky:–
So this wing'd hour is dropt to us from above.
Oh! Clasp we to our hearts, for deathless dower,
This close-companioned inarticulate hour
When twofold silence was the song of love.

> *All Rossetti's senses are sharpened and altered by*
> *his new found ecstasy. Love, to coin a phrase,*
> *changes everything.*

from Uneasy Money
P. G. Wodehouse (1881–1975)

ELIZABETH   Bill, are you really fond of me?

BILL   Fond of you!

> *(Elizabeth sighs.)*

BILL   She gave a sigh.

ELIZABETH   You're so splendid!

BILL   Bill was staggered. Those were strange words. He had
never thought much of himself. He had always looked on
himself as rather a chump – well meaning, perhaps, but an
awful ass! It seemed incredible that anyone, and Elizabeth of
all people, could look on him as splendid.

And yet the very fact that she *had* said it, gave it a plausible sort of sound. It shook his convictions.

ELIZABETH   Splendid!

BILL   Was he? By Jove, perhaps he was, what? Rum idea, but it grew on a chap. Filled with a novel feeling of exultation, he kissed Elizabeth eleven times in rapid succession.

ELIZABETH   Oh, Bill!

BILL   He felt devilish fit. He would have liked to run a mile or two and jump a few gates. He felt grand and strong and full of beans. What a ripping thing life was when you came to think of it.

'She tells her love while half-asleep'

Robert Graves (1895–1985)

She tells her love while half-asleep,
In the dark hours,
With half-words whispered low:
As Earth stirs in her winter sleep
And puts out grass and flowers
Despite the snow
Despite the falling snow.

the tendancy of skin

Aonghas MacNeacail (b. 1942)

the tendancy of skin
to be fine as
pale dog-rose or rich
as ear of corn
to pulse with
yes or hint
that heart-deep there is
fire   sweet hell
for such as cannot
read the membrane's message
clearly   but
in lightly kissing you
i knew
though thought could not have shaped the word
your skin said 'come'.

from Lullaby
W. H. Auden (1907–1973)

Lay your sleeping head, my love,
Human on my faithless arm;
Time and fevers burn away
Individual beauty from
Thoughtful children, and the grave
Proves the child ephemeral:
But in my arms till break of day
Let the living creature lie,
Mortal, guilty, but to me
The entirely beautiful.

Soul and body have no bounds:
To lovers as they lie upon
Her tolerant enchanted shape
In their ordinary swoon,
Aware the vision Venus sends
Of supernatural sympathy,
Universal love and hope;
While an abstract insight wakes
Among the glaciers and the rocks
The hermit's sensual ecstasy.

Juliet
Hilaire Belloc (1870–1953)

How did the party go in Portman Square?
I cannot tell you; Juliet was not there.
And how did Lady Gaster's party go?
Juliet was next me and I do not know.

Going Wrong

The False Heart
Hilaire Belloc (1870–1953)

I said to Heart, "How goes it?" Heart replied:
"Right as a Ribstone Pippin!" But it lied.

And Belloc's heart sounds the first warning note, the discordant note of uncertainty when things start to go wrong. In the next extract, from Howard Barker's play, The Castle, *its heroine, Skinner, is raw with doubts and fears. The play is set at the time of the Crusades, and all the men have long since left the country, leaving it to be governed solely by the women. Skinner, a witch, has become the lover of Ann, the Queen, but here the men are about to return home to reclaim their land and their women, and amongst them is Ann's husband.*

from The Castle
Howard Barker (b. 1947)

SKINNER ... You are very cold this evening, I am not imagining it,
you'll say I'm imagining it, but –

ANN   Yes. *(Pause)*

SKINNER   What, then. *(ANN does not reply.)* They talk of a love-life,
don't they? Do you know the phrase 'love-life', as if
somehow this thing ran under or beside, as if you stepped
from one life to the other, banality to love, love to banality,
no, love is in the cooking and the washing and the milking,
no matter what, the colour of the love stains everything, I say
so anyway, being admittedly of a most peculiar disposition **I
would rather you were dead than took a step or shuffle back
from me**. Dead, and I would do it. There I go, **what is it you
look so distant**.

ANN   I think you are – obsessive. *(Pause)*

SKINNER   Obsessive, me? Obsessive? *(Pause. She fights down
something.)* I nearly got angry, then and nearly went – no – I
will not – and – wait, the anger sinks – *(Pause)* Like tipping
water on the sand, the anger goes, the anger vanishes – into
what? I've no idea, my entrails, I assume. I do piss anger in
the night, my pot is angerfull. *(Pause)* I am obsessive, why
aren't you? *(Pause)* Every stone they raise is aimed at us. And
things we have not dreamed of yet will come from it. Poems,
love and gardening will be – and where you turn your eyes
will be – and even the little middle of your heart which you
think is your safe and actual self will be – transformed by it. I
don't know how but even the way you plait your hair will be
determined by it, and what we crop and even the colour of
the babies, I do think it's odd, so odd, that when you resist
you are obsessive but when you succumb you are not **whose
obsession is this thing** or did you mean my love, they are the
same thing actually. *(Pause)* . . .

Similar theme, but a very different tone, from
P. G. Wodehouse again . . .

The Gourmet's Love-Song

P. G. Wodehouse (1881–1975)

How strange is Love; I am not one
Who Cupid's power belittles,
For Cupid 'tis who makes me shun
My customary victuals.
Oh, EFFIE, since that painful scene
That left me broken-hearted,
My appetite, erstwhile so keen,
Has utterly departed.

My form, my friends observe with pain,
Is growing daily thinner.
Love only occupies the brain
That once could think of dinner.
Around me myriad waiters flit,
With meat and drink to ply men;
Alone, disconsolate, I sit,
And feed on thoughts of Hymen.

The kindly waiters hear my groan,
They strive to charm with curry;
They tempt me with a devilled bone –
I beg them not to worry.
Soup, whitebait, entrees, fricassees,
They bring me uninvited.
I need them not, for what are these
To one whose life is blighted?

They show me dishes rich and rare,
But ah! my pulse no joy stirs.
For savouries I've ceased to care,
I hate the thought of oysters.
They bring me roast, they bring me boiled,
But all in vain they woo me;
The waiters softly mutter, "Foiled!"
The chef, poor man, looks gloomy.

So, EFFIE, turn that shell-like ear,
Nor to my sighing close it,
You cannot doubt that I'm sincere –
This ballad surely shows it.
No longer spurn the suit I press,
Respect my agitation,
Do change your mind, and answer, "Yes",
And save me from starvation.

*Unrequited or frustrated love is often objectively
comic and subjectively tragic, simultaneously.
It's probably true that nobody writes better about
this than Shakespeare, who returns to the theme
endlessly. Here, he extends the scale of the agony
by writing not for one voice, but four.*

from As You Like It

William Shakespeare (1564–1616)

Act V scene ii

PHEBE   Good shepherd, tell this youth what 'tis to love.

SILVIUS   It is to be all made of sighs and tears,
            And so am I for Phebe.

PHEBE   And I for Ganymede.

ORLANDO   And I for Rosalind.

ROSALIND   And I for no woman.

SILVIUS   It is to be all made of faith and service,
            And so am I for Phebe.

PHEBE   And I for Ganymede.

ORLANDO   And I for Rosalind.

ROSALIND   And I for no woman.

SILVIUS   It is to be all made of fantasy,
            All made of passion and all made of wishes,
            All adoration, duty and observance,
            All humbleness, all patience and impatience,
            All purity, all trial, all observance;
            And so am I for Phebe.

PHEBE   And so am I for Ganymede.

ORLANDO   And so am I for Rosalind.

ROSALIND   And so am I for no woman

PHEBE   *(to ROSALIND)* If this be so, why blame you me to love
            you?

SILVIUS   *(to PHEBE)* If this be so, why blame you me to love
            you?

ORLANDO   If this be so, why blame you me to love you?

ROSALIND   Who do you speak to, "Why blame you me to love
            you"?

ORLANDO   To her that is not here, nor doth not hear.

ROSALIND   Pray you, no more of this; 'tis like the howling of
            Irish wolves against the moon.

And here, we took an interval, which involved
refreshments, recrimination and re-writing.
Plus a bout of back-slapping before Part Two.

Part Two

Marriage in Prospect

Four Poems by Dorothy Parker
(1893–1967)

Experience

Some men break your heart in two,
    Some men fawn and flatter,
Some men never look at you;
    And that cleans up the matter.

Unfortunate Coincidence

By the time you swear you're his,
Shivering and sighing,
And he vows his passion is
Infinite, undying –
Lady, make a note of this:
One of you is lying.

Social Note

Lady, lady, should you meet
One whose ways are all discreet,
One who murmurs that his wife
Is the lodestar of his life,
One who keeps assuring you
That he never was untrue,
Never loved another one . . ,
Lady, lady, better run!

Comment

Oh, life is a glorious cycle of song,
A medley of extemporanea;
And love is a thing that can never go wrong;
And I am Marie of Roumania.

*Well, of course she's not British, but we wanted
to include some Dorothy Parker, so we just
cheated. After the confusions, joys and miseries
of young love, it is arguably time to grow up and
settle down. (At time of writing, neither author
of this book has taken their own advice.) This
often means marriage.*
*This Restoration couple, Millament and
Mirabell, are going to go up the aisle with their
eyes wide open . . .*

from The Way of the World
William Congreve (1670–1729)

MILLAMENT   Oh, I hate a lover that can dare to think he draws a
    moment's air independent on the bounty of his mistress.
    There is not so impudent a thing in nature as the saucy look
    of an assured man, confident of success. The pedantic
    arrogance of a very husband has not so pragmatical an air.
    Ah, I'll never marry unless I am first made sure of my will
    and pleasure.

MIRABELL   Would you have 'em both before marriage? Or will
    you be contented with the first now, and stay for the other
    till after grace?

MILLAMENT   Ah, don't be impertinent. My dear liberty, shall I
    leave thee? My faithful solitude, my darling contemplation,
    must I bid you then adieu? Ay-h, adieu. My morning
    thoughts, agreeable wakings, indolent slumbers, all ye
    douceurs, ye sommeils du matin, adieu. I can't do't; 'tis
    more than impossible. Positively, Mirabell, I'll lie abed in a
    morning as long as I please.

MIRABELL   Then I'll get up in a morning as early as I please.

MILLAMENT   Ah, idle creature, get up when you will. And, d'ye
    hear, I won't be called names after I'm married; positively, I
    won't be called names.

MIRABELL   Names?

MILLAMENT   Ay, as wife, spouse, my dear, joy, jewel, love,
    sweetheart, and the rest of that nauseous cant, in which men
    and their wives are so fulsomely familiar. I shall never bear
    that. Good Mirabell, don't let us be familiar or fond, nor
    kiss before folks, like my Lady Fadler and Sir Francis; nor go
    to Hyde Park together the first Sunday in a new chariot, to
    provoke eyes and whispers; and then never be seen there
    together again, as if we were proud of one another the first
    week and ashamed of one another ever after. Let us never
    visit together, nor go to a play together, but let us be very
    strange and well-bred. Let us be as strange as if we had been
    married a great while, and as well-bred as if we were not
    married at all.

MIRABELL   Have you any more conditions to offer? Hitherto
    your demands are pretty reasonable.

MILLAMENT   Trifles! – As liberty to pay and receive visits to and
    from whom I please, to write and receive letters, without
    interrogatories or wry faces on your part. To wear what I
    please, and choose conversation with regard only to my own
    taste. To have no obligation upon me to converse with wits
    that I don't like, because they are your acquaintance, or to
    be intimate with fools because they may be your relations.
    Come to dinner when I please, dine in my dressing-room
    when I'm out of humour, without giving a reason. To have
    my closet inviolate. To be sole empress of my tea-table,
    which you must never presume to approach without first
    asking leave. And lastly, wherever I am, you shall always
    knock at the door before you come in. These articles
    subscribed, if I continue to endure you a little longer, I may
    by degrees dwindle into a wife.

MIRABELL   Your bill of fare is something advanced in this latter
    account. Well, have I liberty to offer conditions, that when
    you are dwindled into a wife, I may not be beyond measure
    enlarged into a husband?

MILLAMENT   You have free leave. Propose your utmost; speak
    and spare not.

MIRABELL   I thank you. Imprimis then: I covenant that your
    acquantance be general; that you admit no sworn
    confidante or intimate of your own sex; no she-friend to
    screen her affairs under your countenance and tempt you to
    make trial of a mutual secrecy.

MILLAMENT   Detestable imprimis!

MIRABELL   Item: I article that you continue to like your own
    face as long as I shall; and while it passes current with me,
    that you endeavour not to new-coin it. To which end,
    together with all vizards for the day, I prohibit all masks for
    the night, made of oiled skins and I know not what – hog's
    bones, hare's gall, pig-water, and the marrow of a roasted
    cat. In short, I forbid all commerce with the gentlewoman in
    what-d'ye-call-it Court. Item: When you shall be breeding –

MILLAMENT   Ah, name it not.

MIRABELL   Which may be presumed, with a blessing on our
    endeavours –

MILLAMENT   Odious endeavours!

MIRABELL   I denounce against all strait-lacing, squeezing for a
    shape till you mould my boy's head like a sugar-loaf, and
    instead of a man-child, make me father to a crooked billet.
    Lastly, to the dominion of the tea-table I submit, but with
    proviso that you exceed not in your province, but restrain
    yourself to native and simple tea-table drinks, as tea,
    chocolate, and coffee. As likewise to genuine and authorised
    tea-table talk, such as mending of fashions, spoiling
    reputations, railing at absent friends, and so forth; but that
    on no account you encroach upon the men's prerogative,
    and presume to drink healths or toast fellows; for
    prevention of which, I banish all foreign forces, all
    auxiliaries to the tea-table, as orange brandy, all aniseed,
    cinnamon, citron, and Barbadoes waters. But for cowslip-
    wine, poppy-water, and all dormitives, those I allow. – These
    provisos admitted, in other things I may prove a tractable
    and complying husband.

MILLAMENT   O horrid provisos! Filthy strong waters! I toast
    fellows, odious men! I hate your odious provisos.

MIRABELL   Then we're agreed. Shall I kiss your hand upon the
    contract?

Young Love: Two

Victoria Wood

GAIL   Carl?

CARL   What?

GAIL   Do you know the facts of life?

CARL   Some of them.

GAIL   Which ones do you know?

CARL   Gravy. I know how that's made. I know where my mam's apron is.

GAIL   Do you know where babies come from?

CARL   'Course I do. They come from women.

GAIL   Yeah, but how come?

CARL   Don't ask me. You want to send off for a pamphlet.

GAIL   What's that?

CARL   They tell you what's what. We've got one at home about lagging.

GAIL   Well, can I not just read yours then, and not send off?

CARL   No, you want a, er, wotsit pamphlet.

GAIL   What?

CARL   You know – 'at it'. What is it you want to know anyway?

GAIL   Well it were something me mam said about my honeymoon.

CARL   What?

GAIL   She said I've not to wear my pixie-hood in bed. She said men don't like it.

CARL   Won't bother me.

GAIL   Will it not, Carl? And you know I always sleep in a Pac-a-mac.

CARL   So what?

GAIL   Do you really not mind, Carl?

CARL   Why should I? I'm not going to be there, am I?

GAIL   In the honeymoon?

CARL   Well, it's the money, in't it, Gail? We can't both go. You go this year, I'll go next.

GAIL   All right, Carl.

In the Room of the Bride-Elect
Thomas Hardy (1840–1928)

"Would it had been the man of our wish!"
Sighs her mother. To whom with vehemence she
In the wedding-dress – the wife to be –
"Then why were you so mollyish
As not to insist on him for me!"
The mother, amazed: "Why, dearest one,
Because you pleaded for this or none!"

"But Father and you should have stood out strong!
Since then, to my cost, I have lived to find
That you were right and that I was wrong:
This man is a dolt to the one declined . . .
Ah! – here he comes with his button-hole rose.
Good God – I must marry him I suppose!"

from In a Doctor's Surgery
Victoria Wood

(*Doctor's waiting room. Pam sits reading* Brides *magazine.*)

CORIN (*Voice Over*) With Pam's marriage to Donald only a week away, she feels the time is right for a little chat with the doctor.

(*The surgery door opens. A man is ushered out by the doctor, frothing at the mouth, bouncing against the walls like a mad moth.*)

DOCTOR As I say, Jim, some people do get a very slight reaction with that one – enjoy your holiday anyway. Miss Twill?

(*Pam steps over the man who is now staggering to the door on all fours.*)

(*Surgery.*)

PAM – so I just wanted a little chat before the wedding night, Doctor.

DOCTOR Very sensible. What about?

PAM Well, I've never had physical fill-fullment, and I thought I'd just pop in and get the gen, Doctor.

DOCTOR Very wise. Well it's quite simple. The woman has an egg in her waterworks, and this comes to an arrangement with the man's plumbing, and Bob's your uncle. (*Standing up*) Any problems, just pop back and see me.

PAM Thank you, Doctor.

Marriage in Reality

"To My Dear and Loving Husband"
Anne Bradstreet (1612–1672)

If ever two were one, then surely we.
If ever man were lov'd by wife, then thee;
If ever wife was happy in a man,
Compare with me ye women if you can.
I prize thy love more than whole Mines of gold,
Or all the riches that the East doth hold.
My love is such that Rivers cannot quench,
Nor ought but love from thee, give recompence.
Thy love is such I can no way repay,
The heavens reward thee manifold I pray.
Then while we live, in love lets so persever,
That when we live no more, we may live ever.

'Reader, I married him' is usually the end of the story. But of course, it's barely half way through. It seems to be an Institution designed, at least in part, to shelter us from the storms of passion and experimentation but in reality marriage turns out to be a prison as often as a haven.

Major Macroo
Stevie Smith   (1902–1971)

Major Hawkaby Cole Macroo
Chose
Very wisely
A patient Griselda of a wife with a heart of gold
That never beat for a soul but him
Himself and his slightest whim.

He left her alone for months at a time
When he had to have a change
Just had to
And his pension wouldn't stretch to a fare for two
And he didn't want it to.
And if she wept she was game and nobody knew it
And she stood at the edge of the tunnel and waved as his train
        went through it.

And because it was cheaper they lived abroad
And did he care if she might be unhappy or bored?
He did not.
He'd other things to think of – a lot.

He'd fads and he fed them fat,
And she could lump it and that was that.

He'd several boy friends
And she thought it was nice for him to have them,
And she loved him and felt that he needed her and waited
And waited and never became exasperated.

Even his room
Was dusted and kept the same,
And when friends came
They went into every room in the house but that one
Which Hawkaby wouldn't have shown.

Such men as these, such selfish cruel men
Hurting what most they love what most loves them,
Never make a mistake when it comes to choosing a woman
To cherish them and be neglected and not think it inhuman.

*Major Macroo has married to provide himself
with an unpaid servant. There are, of course,
many and varied other reasons for getting
hitched – and very often reasons that are given
bear no relation to reasons that have driven. In
Alan Bennett's play* Habeas Corpus, *Lady
Rumpers – a pillar of the establishment – has
discovered that her daughter, Felicity, is
expecting a child out of wedlock. The crisis serves
as a catalyst for Lady Rumpers' revelations abut
her own slightly less-than-spotless history*

from Habeas Corpus
Alan Bennett (b. 1934)

LADY RUMPERS   Many years ago, when I was not much older
    than Felicity is now, I had just arrived in the colonies . . . I . .
    . you have to know this Felicity. I should have told you
    before. I had just arrived in the colonies when I found I was
    P-R-E-G-N-A-N-T.

THROBBING   PRAGNANT?

MRS WICKSTEED   Pegnat.

LADY RUMPERS   PREGNANT. I was not married at the time.

MRS WICKSTEED   What about General Rumpers?

LADY RUMPERS   Tiger and I met soon afterwards. He loved me
    . . . I . . . respected him. We married. He was a gentleman
    but shy. He only went into the Army in order to put his
    moustache to good purpose. He was glad of a child for his
    life too had its secrets: a passing-out party at Sandhurst had
    left him forever incapable of having children. He threw the
    blanket of his name over Felicity and together we achieved
    respectability. Call me fool, call me slut, call me anything
    you like. But I vowed at that time that the same thing should
    never happen to Felicity. And now it has. My poor child. Oh
    Felicity, Felicity.

WICKSTEED   And where is he now, her real father?

LADY RUMPERS   Do you think I have not asked myself that
    question? Lying under mosquito nets in Government House
    do you think that question has not hammered itself into my
    brain?

WICKSTEED   Have you any clues?

LADY RUMPERS   One and one only. He was a doctor. Yes. That is
    why I despise your profession.

MRS WICKSTEED   His name. Do you not know that?

LADY RUMPERS   No. I suppose that shocks you.

MRS WICKSTEED   Nothing could shock me any more.

LADY RUMPERS   Picture the scene. Liverpool. The blitz at its
    height. I am bound for the Far East. Our convoy is
    assembled ready to go down the Mersey on the morning
    tide. Suddenly I am told I cannot sail.

WICKSTEED   Yes?

LADY RUMPERS   No. I had no vaccination certificate. The black-out. An air-raid in progress. The docks ablaze. I set off alone to find a doctor. Buildings crashing all round me. Crash, crash, crash. Bombs raining down on the street. Boom, boom, boom. I see a brass plate. The surgery in darkness. The doctor under the table. He writes me a certificate. I am grateful. Think how grateful I was. We talk.

THROBBING   Yes, yes, go on.

LADY RUMPERS   Two voices in the darkness of the surgery as the storm rages outside. His hand steals into mine . . .

THROBBING   Yes, then what did he do? . . .

LADY RUMPERS   We cling to each other as the bombs fell.

THROBBING   Yes?

LADY RUMPERS   I need not tell you the rest.

THROBBING   They always miss out the best bits.

LADY RUMPERS   The All Clear sounds as I stumble back on board. Came the dawn we clipped out of the Mersey and headed for the open sea. Do you know the Atlantic at all?

MRS WICKSTEED   No.

LADY RUMPERS   It is very rough. I thought I was sea sick. Only when we docked did I realize I had a bun in the club.

MRS WICKSTEED   Tragic.

WICKSTEED   Wonderful.

LADY RUMPERS   I blame the War.

WICKSTEED   Ah the War, that was a strange and wonderful time.
Oh Mavis and Audrey and Lilian and Jean
Patricia and Pauline and NAAFI Christine
Maureen and Myrtle I had you and more
In God's gift to the lecher the Second World War.

MRS SWABB   In shelters and bunkers on Nissen hut floors,
They wrestled with webbing and cellular drawers.
From pillbox on headland they scoured the seas
While pinching our bottoms and stroking our knees.

LADY RUMPERS   Echoes of music drift into the night.
Never in peace will it all seem so right.

WICKSTEED   Oh Lost Generation where are you now?
I still see Lemira, Yvonne's in Slough.
Mothers like you, with girls in their twenties.
Fathers like me: we all share such memories.

LADY RUMPERS   One mad magenta moment and I have paid for it all my life.

Chekhov said: 'If you are afraid of loneliness, don't marry.' These next five extracts touch on this, but also on the great fulfilment and familiarity brought by a long relationship.

The Wife's Poem

Beatrice Hawley

The animals are asleep,
the children are covered,
the mother is standing in the hall
leaning her arms into the sky,
She can't sleep. She watches
the dark spaces crack with light.

The husband is moaning.
He is having a nightmare about lions.
Her hand is there, soothing
him over to a dream of water.
She knows this will not last:
she will break or learn to sleep.

Her hand in the future will be settling
small things down in their corners,
folding a narrow blanket,
hemming thin curtains
for the room with one window only
she will live in alone.

from The Child in Time
Ian McEwan (b. 1948)

The novelty of seeing and feeling a familiar naked body was such
that for some minutes they could do little more than hold each
other at arm's length and say, "Well . . ." and "Here we are
again . . ." A wild jokiness hung in the air, a suppressed hilarity
that threatened to obliterate desire. All the coolness between
them now seemed an elaborate hoax, and they wondered how
they had kept it going for so long. It was amusingly simple: they
had to do no more than remove their clothes and look at one
another to be set free and assume the uncomplicated roles in
which they could not deny their mutual understanding. Now
they were their old, wise selves and they could not stop grinning.

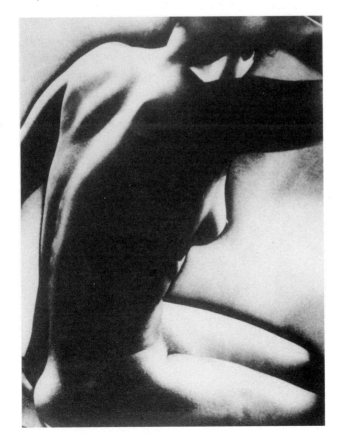

Later, one word seemed to repeat itself as the long-lipped opening parted and closed around him as he filled the known dip and curve and arrived at a deep, familiar place, a smooth resonating word generated by slippery flesh on flesh, a warm humming, softly consonated, roundly vowelled word . . . home, he was home, enclosed, safe and therefore able to provide, home where he owned and was owned. Home, why be anywhere else? Wasn't it wasteful to be doing anything other than this? Time was redeemed, time assumed purpose all over again because it was the medium for the fulfillment of desire. The trees outside edged in closer, needles stroked the small panes, darkening the room which rippled with the movement of filtered light. Heavier rain sounded on the roof and later receded. Julie was crying. He wondered, as he had many times before, how anything so good and simple could be permitted, how they were allowed to get away with it, how the world could have taken this experience into account for so long and still be the way it was. Not governments, or publicity firms or research departments, but biology, existence, matter itself, had dreamed this up for its own pleasure and perpetuity, and this was exactly what you were meant to do, it wanted you to like it. His arms and legs were drifting away. High, in clean air, he hung by his fingers from a mountain ledge; fifty feet below was the long smooth scree. His grip was loosening. Surely then, he thought as he fell backwards into the exquisite dizzy emptiness and accelerated down the irresponsibly steep slope, surely at heart the place is benevolent, it likes us, it wants us to like it, it likes itself.

Two Sonnets
Elizabeth Barrett Browning (1806–1861)

My own Beloved, who has lifted me
From this drear flat of earth where I was thrown
And in betwixt the languid ringlets, blown
A life-breath, till the forehead hopefully
Shines out again, as all the angels see,
Before thy saving kiss! My own, my own,
Who camest to me when the world was gone.
And I who looked for only God, found *thee*!
I find thee: I am safe, and strong, and glad.
As one who stands in dewless asphodel
Looks backward on the tedious time he had
In the upper life . . . so I, with bosom-swell,
Make witness here between the good and bad,
That Love, as strong as Death, retrieves as well.

SONNET XXVII

How do I love thee? Let me count the ways.
I love thee to the depth and breadth and height
My soul can reach, when feeling out of sight
For the ends of Being and Ideal Grace.
I love thee to the level of everyday's
Most quiet need, by sun and candlelight.
I love thee freely, as men strive for Right;
I love thee purely, as they turn from Praise;
I love thee with the passion put to use
In my old griefs, and with my childhood's faith;
I love with a love I seemed to lose
With my lost saints, – I love thee with the breath,
Smiles, tears, of all my life! – and, if God choose,
I shall but love thee better after death.

SONNET XLII

Les Sylphides
Louis MacNeice (1907–1963)

Life in a day: he took his girl to the ballet;
Being shortsighted himself could hardly see it –
> The white skirts in the grey
> Glade and the swell of the music
> Lifting the white sails.

Calyx upon calyx, canterbury bells in the breeze
The flowers on the left mirror to the flowers on the right
> And the naked arms above
> The powdered faces moving
> Like seaweed in a pool.

Now, he thought, we are floating – ageless, oarless –
Now there is no separation, from now on
> You will be wearing white
> Satin and a red sash
> Under the waltzing trees.

But the music stopped, the dancers took their curtain,
The river had come to a lock – a shuffle of programmes –
> And we cannot continue down
> Stream unless we are ready
> To enter the lock and drop.

So they were married – to be the more together –
And found they were never again so much together,
> Divided by the morning tea,
> By the evening paper,
> By children and tradesmen's bills.

Waking at times in the night she found assurance
Due to his regular breathing but wondered whether
> It was really worth it and where
> The river had flowed away
> And where were the white flowers.

And it is often the case, that in feeling the loss of
MacNeice's 'white flowers', we seek to find them
again, and in doing so, wander into the garden
of temptation.

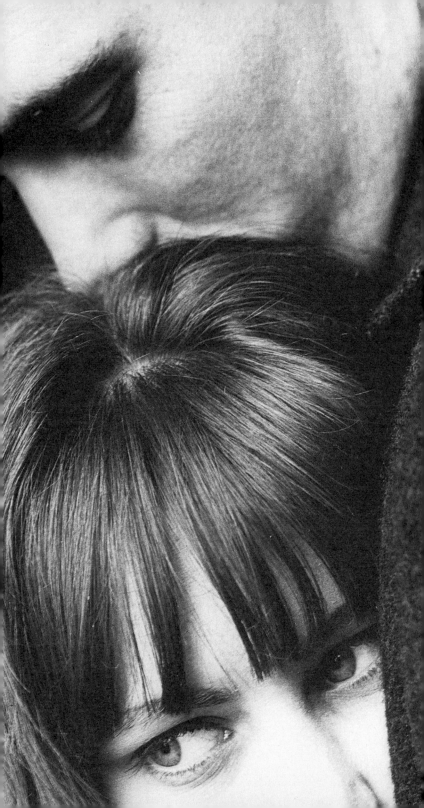

Looking Elsewhere

Adultery Song
Liz Lochhead (b. 1947)

Chorus
I am nothing
To write home about
I am the best thing in your life
But I am best kept secret
From the kids and the wife

We keep each other's counsel
Find our new confidences sweet,
Ignore each other in crowded rooms
Where even our eyes can't meet. –
Till sick of feeling love sick
We seek temporary cures
Always my place
Never yours.

Chorus
Because I am nothing
To write home about
I am the best thing in your life
But I am best kept secret
From the kids and the wife

We talk of somewhere we'll go sometime
As soon as you can –
Till then I'm snatching stolen time
With a borrowed man.
We salt our suppers with secrecy,
Steal kisses in the park
Then you love me half the night with the light on –
But you keep her in the dark.

Chorus
No I am nothing
To write home about
I am the best thing in your life
But you have to keep me secret
From the kids and the wife

You say you're sorry to leave me
I say it is OK
And skin to skin we cling once more
Then you shower love away,
Take the car keys by my ticking clock
go and leave me in my bed
with her photo in your wallet –
my phone number in your head.

Chorus
Cause there's nothing
I could phone your home about –
there's the kids and the wife
even for a matter of life and death
I can't interrupt your life

Chorus
No I am nothing
to write home about
I am the best thing in your life
but I am best kept secret
from the kids and the wife

Now, in another scene from Habeas Corpus, *Shanks, a false breast salesman, encounters Muriel Wicksteed, who is trapped in a loveless marriage. He assumes she is wearing two of his products. She is not.*

from Habeas Corpus

Alan Bennett (b. 1934)

(Enter Mr Shanks.)

MRS WICKSTEED   Percy . . . Oh, good afternoon.

SHANKS   I'm looking for someone by the name of Wicksteed.
W-I-C-K-S-T-E-E-D. Wicksteed. Yes.

MRS WICKSTEED   Yes?

SHANKS   And I think I've found her. Mr Shanks is the name.
Full marks. Ten out of ten. They are wonderful. *Wonderful.*

MRS WICKSTEED   You think so?

SHANKS   They are outstanding. Out-standing.

MRS WICKSTEED   Golly. Appreciation after all these years.

SHANKS   What a charming home, and my goodness, don't they
enhance it. The balance, dear lady, almost perfection.
Almost, but not quite. Still, that's what I'm here for. May I?

MRS WICKSTEED   This is what they must mean by the Permissive
Society.

SHANKS   I believe this one is a fraction bigger than the other.

MRS WICKSTEED   To hell with symmetry. How that touch revives
me.

SHANKS   It will not have escaped your notice that the customer,
Miss Wicksteed, is becoming a little excited.

MRS WICKSTEED   At last! A tenant for my fallow loins.

SHANKS   However, rest assured. This excitement is not mutual. I
am an expert. A crash course at Leatherhead, the firm's
training centre, set in the heart of Surrey's famous rural
surroundings, lays down a standard procedure for every
eventuality. Mind you, these are exceptional. I've only seen
one pair to rival these, and she's now the manageress of the
only cinema in Fleetwood. Look, you're such an outstanding
example, we often compare notes, my colleagues and I . . .
and since I've got my little Polaroid handy . . .

MRS WICKSTEED   I was wondering when you were going to
mention that. Your Polaroid, your lovely little Polaroid . . .

SHANKS   Some snaps . . . just for the record . . .

MRS WICKSTEED   Yes, yes, a record. Music!

(The stage is flooded with sensual music.)

Muriel Wicksteed, what are you doing? Can this be you? Yes. Yes, it is me. The real me. The me I've always been deep down. Suddenly the body reasserts itself, breaks through the dead crust of morality, and from the chrysalis convention bursts the butterfly, freedom.

(The telephone rings.)

I will see to that. Dr Wicksteed's residence. Oh, it's you Mr Purdue. No, you cannot speak to Dr Wicksteed. This is his afternoon off. You're about to commit suicide? I see. If you must choose to commit suicide on doctor's afternoon off, that's your funeral. Au revoir. Or I suppose I should say good-bye. Now where was I . . . Oh yes.

(She embraces Shanks.)

SHANKS   I repeat there is nothing to be ashamed of. This is all in a day's work to me.

MRS WICKSTEED   I don't think he should throw his promiscuity in my face. One doesn't like to think one is simply a convenience.

SHANKS   A client, not a convenience.

MRS WICKSTEED   Client? I'm not going to have to pay you for this?

SHANKS   It's all included in the five pounds.

MRS WICKSTEED   Five pounds! That's wicked.

SHANKS   There's nothing more I can do.

MRS WICKSTEED   He comes in here, goes for my bust like a bull at a gate and then says there's nothing more he can do. There is more. 'The bust is but the first port of call on the long voyage of love.'

SHANKS   I have other ladies to see.

MRS WICKSTEED   Other ladies. The idea!

SHANKS   Stop. Take them off. They are a sacred trust. You are not fit to wear them.

(He slaps her bust)

SHANKS   It's the . . . it's the real thing, isn't it? Flesh.

MRS WICKSTEED   Of course it's flesh. What did you think it was – blancmange?

SHANKS   Is there anywhere I could wash my hands?

MRS WICKSTEED   Time enough to wash your hands when we've
    been to Paradise and back.
SHANKS   No!
MRS WICKSTEED   No. That means yes. So much at least Freud
    has taught us.

At Lunchtime – A Story of Love

Roger McGough (b. 1937)

When the busstopped suddenly to avoid
damaging a mother and child in the road, the
younglady in the greenhat sitting opposite
was thrown across me, and not being one to
miss an opportunity i started to makelove
with all my body.

At first she resisted saying that it
was tooearly in the morning and toosoon
after breakfast and that anyway she found
me repulsive. But when i explained that
this being a nuclearage, the world was going
to end at lunchtime, she took off her
greenhat, put her busticket in her pocket
and joined in the exercise.

The buspeople, and therewere many of
them, were shockedandsurprised and amused
andannoyed, but when the word got around
that the world was coming to an end at lunchtime, they put their pride in their pockets
with their bustickets and madelove one with
the other. And even the busconductor,
climbed into the cab and struck up
some sort of relationship with the driver.

Thatnight, on the bus coming home,
wewere all a little embarrassed, especially me
and the younglady in the greenhat, and we
all started to say in different ways howhasty
and foolish we had been. Butthen, always
having been a bitofalad, i stood up and
said it was a pity that the world didn't nearly
end every lunchtime and that we could always
pretend. And then it happened . . .

Quick as a crash we all changed partners
and soon the bus was a quiver with white
mothballbodies doing naughty things.

And the next day
And everyday
In everybus
In everystreet
In everytown
In everycountry

people pretended that the world was coming
to an end at lunchtime. It still hasn't
Although in a way it has.

'Sexual intercourse began in 1963
Between the end of the Chatterley ban
And the Beatles' first L.P.'

So wrote Philip Larkin back in the 1970s – but of course it didn't.
Debate as to what marriage should and should not be has raged on for
centuries. Dora Russell, second wife of Bertrand, here writing about
alternatives in 1925 . . .

from Hypatia

Dora Russell (1894–1958)

The plain truth is that there are as many types of lover among
women of all classes as among men, and that nothing but
honesty and freedom will make instinctive satisfaction possible
for all. Grant each man and woman the right to seek his or her
own solution without fear of public censure. Moral questions of
this kind cannot be decided by some abstract rule. It would not
be wrong for a man to have six wives, provided he and they all
found mutual happiness in that arrangement; nor for a woman
to have six husbands and a child by each, if she and they found
such a life satisfactory. The wrong lies in rules that are barriers
between human beings who would otherwise reach a fuller and
more intense understanding of one another. And any man or
woman of intelligence and vitality can testify that to have known
each other as lovers is to have completed mental and spiritual, as
well as physical, understanding, and to have permanently
enriched each other's lives, capacities, energies, imaginations.
There is no need to make these divisions into mind and body.
There is no difference.

And here Mary Wollstonecraft, writing more than two hundred years ago . . .

from A Vindication of the Rights of Women
Mary Wollstonecraft (1759–1797)

Would men but generously snap our chains, and be content with rational fellowship instead of slavish obedience, they would find us more observant daughters, more affectionate sisters, more faithful wives, more reasonable mothers – in a word, better citizens. We should then love them with true affection, because we should learn to respect ourselves; and the peace of mind of a worthy man would not be interrupted by the idle vanity of his wife, nor the babes sent to nestle in a strange bosom, having never found a home in their mother's.

It is vain to expect virtue from women till they are, in some degree, independent of men. Whilst they are absolutely dependent on their husbands they will be cunning, mean, and selfish, and the men who can be gratified by the fawning fondness of spaniel-like affection, have not much delicacy, for love is not to be bought, in any sense of the word; its silken wings are instantly shrivelled up when any thing beside a return in kind is sought.

Alternatives

And a 'return in kind' can come from the most
unexpected quarters, and in many forms. After
all –
'Love looks not with the eyes, but with the mind;
And therefore is winged Cupid painted blind,'
as Shakespeare's Helena says.

Vita Sackville-West had been married to Harold
Nicolson for many years when she met Virginia
Woolf and fell completely in love with her,
remaining so for much of her married life. Here
is one of her letters.

Letter to Virginia Woolf

Vita Sackville-West (1892–1962)

I am reduced to a thing that wants Virginia. I composed a
beautiful letter to you in the sleepless nightmare hours of the
night, and it has all gone: I just miss you, in a quite simple
desperate human way. You, with all your un-dumb letters, would
never write so elementary a phrase as that; perhaps you wouldn't
even feel it. And yet I believe you'll be sensible of a little gap. But
you'd clothe it in so exquisite a phrase that it would lose a little
of its reality. Whereas with me it is quite stark: I miss you even
more than I could have believed; and I was prepared to miss you
a good deal. So this letter is just really a squeal of pain. It is
incredible how essential to me you have become. I suppose you
are accustomed to people saying these things. Damn you, spoilt
creature; I shan't make you love me any the more by giving
myself away like this – But oh my dear, I *can't* be clever and stand-
offish with you: I love you too much for that. Too truly. You have
no idea how stand-offish I can be with people I don't love. I have
brought it to a fine art. But you have broken down my defences.
And I don't really resent it.

Song of a Young Lady to Her Ancient Lover

John Wilmot, Earl of Rochester (1647–1680)

Ancient Person, for whom I
All the flattering Youth defy:
Long be it ere thou grow Old,
Aching, shaking, crazy Cold.
But still continue as thou art,
Ancient Person of my Heart.

On thy wither'd Lips and Dry
Which like barren Furrows lye,
Brooking Kisses I will pour
Shall thy Youthful Heat restore.
Such kind show'rs in Autumn fall,
And a Second Spring recall:
Nor from thee will ever part,
Ancient Person of my Heart.

The Nobler parts which but to name
In our Sex would be counted shame,
By Age's frozen grasp possest,
From their ice shall be releast:
And sooth'd by my reviving hand
In former warmth and vigour stand.
All a lover's wish can reach
For thy Joy my love shall teach.
And for thy Pleasure shall improve
All that Art can add to Love.
Yet still I love thee without Art,
Ancient Person of my Heart.

Freddy

Stevie Smith (1902–1971)

Nobody knows what I feel about Freddy
I cannot make anyone understand
I love him sub specie aeternitatis
I love him out of hand.
I don't love him so much in the restaurants that's a fact
To get him hobnob with my old pub chums needs too much tact
He don't love them and they don't love him
In the pub lub lights they say Freddy very dim.
But get him alone on the open saltings
Where the sea licks up to the fen
He is his and my own heart's best
World without end ahem.
People who say we ought to get married ought to get smacked:
Why should we do it when we can't afford it and have ourselves
        whacked?
Thank you kind friends and relations thank *you,*
We do very well as we do.
Oh what do I care for the pub lub lights
And the friends I love so well –
There's more in the way I feel about Freddy
Than a friend can tell.
But all the same I don't care much for his meelyoo I mean
I don't anheimate mich in the ha-ha well-off suburban scene
Where men are few and hearts go tumptytum
In the tennis club lub lights poet very dumb.
But there never was a boy like Freddy
For a haystack's ivory tower of bliss
Where speaking sub specie humanitatis
Freddy and me can kiss.
Exiled from his meelyoo
Exiled from mine
There's all Tom Tiddler's time pocket
For his love and mine.

Dockery & Son
Philip Larkin (1922–1985)

'Dockery was junior to you,
Wasn't he?' said the Dean. 'His son's here now.'
Death-suited, visitant, I nod. 'And do
You keep in touch with —' O remember how
Black-gowned, unbreakfasted, and still half-tight
We used to stand before that desk, to give
'Our version' of 'these incidents last night'?
I try the door of where I used to live:

Locked. The lawn spreads dazzlingly wide.
A known bell chimes. I catch my train, ignored.
Canal and clouds and colleges subside
Slowly from view. But Dockery, good Lord,
Anyone up today must have been born
In '43, when I was twenty-one.
If he was younger, did he get this son
At nineteen, twenty? Was he that withdrawn

High-collared public-schoolboy, sharing rooms
With Cartwright who was killed? Well, it just shows
How much . . . How little . . . Yawning, I suppose
I fell asleep, waking at the fumes
And furnace-glares of Sheffield, where I changed,
And ate an awful pie, and walked along
The platform to its end to see the ranged
Joining and parting lines reflect a strong

Unhindered moon. To have no son, no wife,
No house or land still seemed quite natural.
Only a numbness registered the shock
Of finding out how much had gone of life,
How widely from the others. Dockery, now:
Only nineteen, he must have taken stock
Of what he wanted, and been capable
Of . . . No, that's not the difference: rather, how

Convinced he was he should be added to!
Why did he think adding meant increase?
To me it was dilution. Where do these
Innate assumptions come from? Not from what
We think truest, or most want to do:
Those warp tight-shut, like doors. They're more a style
Our lives bring with them: habit for a while,
Suddenly they harden into all we've got

And how we got it; looked back on, they rear
Like sand-clouds, thick and close, embodying
For Dockery a son, for me nothing,
Nothing with all a son's harsh patronage.
Life is first boredom, then fear.
Whether or not we use it, it goes,
And leaves what something hidden from us chose,
And age, and then the only end of age.

Love and Loss

Larkin's conclusion is a challengingly bleak one. This section is about bereavement and survival – not love ending necessarily, because it doesn't, but about the experience of love and loss becoming inseparable.

Letter to Harold Nicolson
Vita Sackville-West (1892–1962)

My own darling Hadji

I was thinking this morning how awful it would be if you died. I do often think that; but it came over me all of a heap when I looked out of the bathroom window and saw you in your blue coat and black hat, peering into your scoop*. It is the sort of sudden view of a person that twists one's heart, when they don't know you are observing them – they have an innocent look, almost as a child asleep – one feels one is spying on some secret life one should not know about. Taking advantage as it were, although it is only the most loving advantage that one takes.

Anyway, the scoop would be the most poignant coffee-cup ever made. I often think that I have never told you how much I love you – and if you died I should reproach myself, saying 'Why did I never tell him? Why did I never tell him enough?'

Your Mar

* *'The scoop' was a hollow in one of the paving stones in the Cottage Garden at Sissinghurst, and Harold used it as a rain gauge.*

from A Grief Observed

C. S. Lewis (1898–1963)

And then one or other dies. And we think of this as love cut short; like a dance stopped in mid career or a flower with its head unluckily snapped off – something truncated and therefore, lacking its due shape. I wonder. If, as I can't help suspecting, the dead also feel the pains of separation (and this may be one of their purgatorial sufferings), then for both lovers, and for all pairs of lovers without exception, bereavement is a universal and integral part of our experience of love. It follows marriage as normally as marriage follows courtship or as autumn follows summer. It is not a truncation of the process but one of its phases; not the interruption of the dance, but the next figure. We are 'taken out of ourselves' by the loved one while she is here. Then comes the tragic figure of the dance in which we must learn to be still taken out of ourselves though the bodily presence is withdrawn, to love the very Her, and not fall back to loving our past, or our memory, or our sorrow or our relief from sorrow, or our own love.

Song for Hedli Anderson

W. H. Auden (1907–1973)

Stop all the clocks, cut off the telephone,
Prevent the dog from barking with a juicy bone,
Silence the pianos and with muffled drum
Bring out the coffin, let the mourners come.

Let aeroplanes circle moaning overhead
Scribbling on the sky the message He Is Dead,
Put crepe bows round the white necks of the public doves,
Let the traffic policemen wear black cotton gloves.

He was my North, my South, my East and West,
My working week and my Sunday rest,
My noon, my midnight, my talk, my song;
I thought that love would last for ever: I was wrong.

The stars are not wanted now: put out every one;
Pack up the moon and dismantle the sun;
Pour away the ocean and sweep up the wood.
For nothing now can ever come to any good.

The Kaleidoscope
Douglas Dunn (b. 1942)

To climb these stairs again, bearing a tray,
Might be to find you pillowed with your books,
Your inventories listing gowns and frocks
As if preparing for a holiday.
Or, turning from the landing, I might find
My presence watched through your kaleidoscope,
A symmetry of husbands, each redesigned
In lovely forms of foresight, prayer and hope.
I climb these stairs a dozen times a day
And, by that open door, wait, looking in
At where you died. My hands become a tray
Offering me, my flesh, my soul, my skin.
Grief wrongs us so. I stand, and wait, and cry
For the absurd forgiveness, not knowing why.

Epitaph to Her Husband

Lady Catherine Dyer (fl. 1630)

My dearest dust, could not thy hasty day
Afford thy drowszy patience leave to stay
One hower longer: so that we might either
Sate up, or gone to bedd together?
But since thy finisht labour hath possest
Thy weary limbs with early rest,
Enjoy it sweetly: and thy widdowe bride
Shall soone repose her by thy slumbring side.
Whose business, now, is only to prepare
My nightly dress, and call to prayre:
Mine eyes wax heavy and ye day growes old.
The dew falls thick, my belovd growes cold.
Draw, draw ye closed curtaynes: and make roome:
My dear, my dearest dust; I come, I come.

For Nina, the heroine of Anthony Minghella's film Truly Madly Deeply, *the pain of bereavement is literally unbearable – so her dead lover, Jamie, returns to help her let go of him.*

from Truly Madly Deeply
Anthony Minghella

(The ghosts leave, rather sulkily. Nina and Jamie alone.)

JAMIE   *(furious)* Satisfied?

(Then he sneezes, dramatically, repeatedly.)

NINA   *(acidly)* It's only dust.

JAMIE   Nina, that was really humiliating. You ask people to give you a hand, they don't need to, they lug your furniture around half the day and then you come back and throw a tantrum. That was really really really humiliating.

(He sneezes again. It settles in silence.)

NINA   *(desperate, foundering)* Was it like this before?

JAMIE   *(as he blows his nose)* What?

NINA   Before, were we like this?

JAMIE   What? Like what? Look, you're tired, your friend just had a baby, you were up half the night, it's traumatic, it's an emotional experience, let's not turn that into –

NINA   Tell me about the first night we spent together.

JAMIE   Why? Seriously? You want me to?

NINA   What did we do?

JAMIE   We talked.

NINA   What else?

JAMIE   Well, talking was the major component! Uh, uh, we, you played the piano – and I played and we both played a duet – something, I can't remember . . . and you danced for about three hours until I fell asleep, but you were fantastic! – and then we had some cornflakes and when we kissed – which was about eleven o'clock the following day – we were trembling so much we couldn't take off our clothes.

(They remember. They're both sitting now on the bare boards. Quiet. Closer.)

NINA   You see, I held that baby – so

101

(She makes a tangible gesture.)

It's life, it's a life I want. And, and, and all my taste . . . my things, after you died. I found stuff in my trunk I'd put there because you disapproved or laughed at them – books and photographs and I couldn't, I didn't know how to mend a fuse or find a plumber or bleed a radiator but – and now I do. It is a ridiculous flat, but I'll get there, it'll be beautiful, it could be, I think it could be. I, I, I – I so much longed for you, I longed for you.

JAMIE   How's your Spanish?

NINA   What?

JAMIE   There's a poem I wanted you to translate. I read it, there's a bit that I wanted to tell you, I wanted you to hear –

NINA   Okay.

JAMIE   *(recites an extract from the poem,* The Dead Woman *by Pablo Neruda)*

JAMIE   Uh – *Perdoname.*

NINA   *(translating)* Forgive me.

JAMIE   *Si tu no vives,*

NINA   I know this poem. If you are not living . . .

JAMIE   *Si tu, querida, amor mio*
         Si tu te has muerto

NINA   If you, beloved, my love,
         If you have died

JAMIE   *Todas las hojas caeran en mi pecho*

NINA   All the leaves will fall on my breast

JAMIE   *Llovera sobre mi alma noche y dia*

NINA   It will rain on my soul, all night, all day

JAMIE   *Mis pies querran marchar hacia donde tu duermes*

NINA   My feet will want to march to where you are sleeping
         Your accent's terrible.

JAMIE   *Pero seguire vivo*
         (Nina gets up and goes to Jamie.)

NINA   My feet will want to march to where you are sleeping but I shall go on living.

JAMIE   Do you want me to go?
         (She clings to him)

NINA   No, never, never, never, never, never.

Epilogues
The Serious and The Lighthearted

We end with two epilogues for the price of one. The first is serious, the second lighthearted. Auden's song flings the whole subject up into the air and watches it catch the light – there is a wonderful what-the-hell quality about this delighted bafflement. Larkin's poem is also full of questioning, but the guarded optimism of its ending is a much more cautious affair. Take your pick.

An Arundel Tomb
Philip Larkin (1922–1985)

Side by side, their faces blurred,
The earl and countess lie in stone,
Their proper habits vaguely shown
As jointed armour, stiffened pleat,
And that faint hint of the absurd –
The little dogs under their feet.

Such plainness of the pre-baroque
Hardly involves the eye, until
It meets his left-hand gauntlet, still
Clasped empty in the other; and
One sees, with a sharp tender shock,
His hand withdrawn, holding her hand.

They would not think to lie so long.
Such faithfulness in effigy
Was just a detail friends would see:
A sculptor's sweet commissioned grace
Thrown off in helping to prolong
The Latin names around the base.

They would not guess how early in
Their supine stationary voyage
The air would change to soundless damage,
Turn the old tenantry away;
How soon succeeding eyes begin
To look, not read. Rigidly they

Persisted, linked, through lengths and breadths
Of time. Snow fell, undated. Light
Each summer thronged the glass. A bright
Litter of bird-calls strewed the same
Bone-riddled ground. And up the paths
The endless altered people came,

Washing at their identity.
Now, helpless in the hollow of
An unarmorial age, a trough
Of smoke in slow suspended skeins
Above their scrap of history,
Only an attitude remains:

Time has transfigured them into
Untruth. The stone fidelity
They hardly meant has come to be
Their final blazon, and to prove
Our almost-instinct almost true:
What will survive of us is love.

O Tell Me The Truth About Love
W. H. Auden (1907–1973)

Some say that love's a little boy
      And some say it's a bird,
Some say it makes the world go round,
      And some say that's absurd,
And when I asked the man next-door,
      Who looked as if he knew,
His wife got very cross indeed,
      And said it wouldn't do.

Does it look like a pair of pyjamas,
      Or the ham in a temperance hotel?
Does its odour remind one of llamas,
      Or has it a comforting smell?
Is it prickly to touch as a hedge is,
      Or soft as eiderdown fluff?
Is it sharp or quite smooth at the edges?
      O tell me the truth about love.

Our history books refer to it
      In cryptic little notes
It's quite a common topic on
      The Transatlantic boats;
I've found the subject mentioned in
      Accounts of suicides,
And even seen it scribbled on
      The backs of railway-guides.

Does it howl like a hungry Alsatian,
      Or boom like a military band?
Could one give a first-rate imitation
      On a saw or a Steinway Grand?
Is its singing at parties a riot?
      Does it only like Classical stuff?
Will it stop when one wants to be quiet?
      O tell me the truth about love.

I looked inside the summer-house;
 It wasn't ever there:
I tried the Thames at Maidenhead,
 And Brighton's bracing air.
I don't know what the blackbird sang,
 Or what the tulip said;
But it wasn't in the chicken-run,
 Or underneath the bed.

Can it pull extraordinary faces?
 Is it usually sick on a swing?
Does it spend all its time at the races,
 Or fiddling with pieces of string?
Has it views of its own about money?
 Does it think Patriotism enough?
Are its stories vulgar but funny?
 O tell me the truth about love.

When it comes, will it come without warning
 Just as I'm picking my nose?
Will it knock on my door in the morning
 Or tread in the bus on my toes?
Will it come like a change in the weather?
 Will its greeting be courteous or rough?
Will it alter my life altogether?
 O tell me the truth about love.

Picture Acknowledgments

© **Noya Brandt:** *page 17* Withens

Michael Busselle: *page 51* Woodland Scene

Hulton-Deutsch Collection: *page 13* Somewhere in Britain on Every Day of the War.

Jorge Lewinski/Thames and Hudson: *page 92* Philip Larkin's Hull. A Post-War Sense of Desolation.

The Estate of Man Ray: *page 69* Nu solarisé

Mary Evans Picture Library: *page 20* Starting Young; *page 28* Couple Meeting in a Country Lane; *page 31* The Wrestling Match; *page 37* The Story of Hereward/C. H. Selous; *page 39* Lady Lilith by D. G. Rossetti; *page 41* Loving Hands; *page 43* Hey, Ho, the Wind and the Rain; *page 48* Thoughts of You; *page 53* Lovers in a Soho Cafe/Thurston Hopkins; *page 56* The Marriage Market; *page 73* Discussing her Milliner's Bills; *page 79* The Meeting; *page 85* Convicts and Lunatics Have No Vote for Parliament; *page 93* Oxford: The Dreaming Spires; *page 104* Medieval Knight; *page 107* Love/Grace Robertson.

The Royal Photographic Society, Bath: *page 89* King Lear and his Daughters by Julia Margaret Cameron

Topham: *page 24* Young Men's Impudence; *page 64* Domestic Bliss, about 1860; *page 66* Camp Fence; *page 71* A Young Man's Fancy; *page 74* Young Couple Kissing; *page 81* Sam Widges Coffee Bar, Soho; *page 97* Couples; *page 100* True Love Knot.

A

B

C

D

E

F

G

H